BEYOND THE VEIL

Franciele M. Rossi

To Love—

For the way you shaped me, broke me, and remade me. For the gift of being able to receive you, and the courage to carry you forward, always, until my last day.

If you want to understand me, you have to start with that morning. With him. With us.

PREFACE

This book began with a single, unbearable morning.

I have tried to name what grief does to a life — how it rewires language, memory, even the way a teacup tastes.

I wrote these pages to hold the messy, ordinary moments: the tiny kindnesses, the humiliations, the flashes of joy — alongside the nights that feel like avalanches.

I want you to meet him the way I knew him. Alive. Kind. Present in the music he loved. Stubborn in his laughter. The best version of me was always tied to him.

I also want to be honest about the ways grief keeps teaching me. And about how love — the thing I have been searching for my whole life — does not end when a life does.

Love is the greatest gift of humankind.

Read this book as a conversation. Sometimes I will be raw. Sometimes I will try to make sense. Mostly, I will try to be faithful to the truth of what I hold.

PROLOGUE

January 10, 2024.

8:30am. I woke up. The bed was empty.

I texted him: Baby, where are you?

Something felt wrong. A heaviness. But I closed my eyes and drifted back.

10:15am. No response.

I bolted out of bed. My chest already screaming before my mouth did.

Living room—empty.

My heart pounding so hard I thought it would split me open. I knew. I knew.

Garage.

And there he was.

Squatting against the wall.

Cold. Purple around the lips.

I screamed until my throat tore.

I pulled him to the ground. CPR. Counting, pressing, begging.

Ran. Narcan. Back. Nothing. He didn't move.

Back to CPR. Back to screaming.

No phone. Ran again. Hands shaking so bad I couldn't dial. Couldn't breathe. Couldn't think.

Focus. Just focus. Say the words.

911. "My husband is unconscious. I'm doing CPR. Please—please get here."

The call dropped. I redialed.

I called his brother. Screamed. Hung up. Back to CPR.

I screamed until my neighbors had to hear. Please! Someone help me! Please don't do this to me! Please don't take him. God, please don't take the only thing I love.

His eyes staring. Red. His lips purple. He didn't taste the same. His body was not his body anymore.

I knew. But I couldn't let myself believe it.

Paramedics. They pulled him out to the driveway.

I stood there, watching. The wind on my skin. Birds singing. The warmth of the sun hitting us both like nothing was wrong.

Cruel, ordinary life.

I felt like I had failed him. Failed us.

He looked defeated. Like the demon had won.

I sat there watching my dreams vanish, second by second. With every pump of his chest I saw our life — our first kiss, the first time he told me he loved me, the way it felt to be in his arms, his hugs. Each memory slipping, slowly drifting away.

Every happiness, every love, every desire, every dream — collapsing in front of me, second by second.

He looked peaceful. The sun across his face.

I held on to every flicker, every impossible hope that maybe he'd come back.

But the miracle never came.

They stopped CPR.

Everything inside me went dark.

No tears. Just shock. Just silence.

Now... now what?

When love, is both a gift and a wound, how do
you survive it?

❧

By Franciele M. Rossi

BEYOND THE VEIL

Demons

I am one of three siblings—

an older brother and a younger sister.

As the middle child, there are always things you can get away with.

My mother was always too busy caring for my youngest sister,

or too worried about my older brother.

A mother of three, with little left for herself.

That's all I saw in her eyes every time I came and went:

tired, distracted, never resting.

And so, there I was—

alone in a small house that felt so big at times.

You're too old to be afraid of the dark, she'd tell me.

You're too young for sleepovers, she'd say.

When you grow up in a house full of rules—

but none that truly matter—

you start to wonder.

You start to ask questions.

If God is real, why can the demons under my bed be?

What is good?

Why is that a bad thing?

You ask too many questions, was all I ever heard.

So after a while... I stopped.

I stopped asking.

I stopped wondering.

But the fear grew.

I was afraid of the dark.

And I didn't know why.

What makes a demon a demon?
If they're already here, why should I run?
Why do I always have to run from them?

One day, he came to me—
in a dream too real to be imagined.
He wouldn't let me run.
He caught me.
And I was so innocent...
and so afraid.
Afraid of him,
afraid of myself.

Was it real?
Are you real?
Or was I just dreaming?

We all have demons in some form—
lies we shouldn't tell,

choices we shouldn't make.

You don't have to be a genius to know right from wrong...

and yet we still take the wrong turn sometimes.

Like that soft voice on your shoulder,

whispering promises you know you shouldn't listen to—

but do anyway.

After a while, I grew tired of running.

I figured, if you're here,

and you're not leaving,

then something has to give.

I started to catch you in the corner of my eye.

You were here for a reason.

Here to tell me something.

So I confronted every demon of mine.

I'm no longer afraid.

What do you want from me? I asked.

We can spend our entire lives running from ourselves—

burying our deepest secrets,

too afraid to look into our own eyes,

because sometimes we don't want to see what's hiding behind our lies.

It's easier to point at others.

Easier to look anywhere but within.

But I faced mine.

And I told them:

Tell me something I need to know.

Tell me something I don't know.

You can't hurt me anymore.

Afraid of the dark—

I was.

But not now.

Now, I invite them in.

Not to stay.

Not to haunt me.

Not because I need them.

But because if they're here,

they'd better tell me something I don't know.

The thing about losing the most precious thing in life

is that there's nothing left they can take from you.

There's no bargain to be made.

They can't give me what I need.

And if you're not here to stay,

then speak.

Tell me something I don't know.

If you really look closely,

you can see the demons in the people you love—

greed, power, fame, money.

In a world where nothing real can be bargained,

it becomes a dangerous place.

Vague promises of things I can't carry beyond the veil.

Because the only thing they could offer me,

I've already lost.

Another love, they say—
a true love.
One that will stay.

So clever.
The promise of the only thing I crave most.

But where love lives,
grief lingers.

So I ask again:
Tell me something I don't know.

And maybe that's why I started dreaming so young—
because when you live surrounded by shadows,
you learn to imagine the light.

FATE

What is fate?

Fate is something you can't escape.
You can't fight it.

My whole life, I carried big dreams.
Big hopes.
The fairytale.
The big white house with the white fence.
A dog to love.
Dreams...
dreams were always dreams.

I can't explain how I got here—
was it luck?

Or was it the knowing that I had no other option?

That I had to do what I had to do to get what I needed,

because I knew no one else would be there for me?

I left my parents' house so young,

carrying more dreams than I had years.

My mother used to say,

You dream too big, who do you think you are?

But what is life without dreams?

I have failed a hundred times—

and I know I will fail a hundred more.

And I have accepted that.

This is my life.

I can't change it.

I won't change it.

In my wildest dreams,

I would never have imagined living the life I've lived.

Or loving the way I have loved.

At times, it feels like I've lived a hundred lives in one.

Was my mother wrong?

Or was I lucky?

It's never about the destination.

It never is.

The worst parts of my life have been my greatest gifts.

I feel so old, and yet so young.

I appreciate life differently now.

I enjoy my slow days.

I don't chase anymore.

I have spent too many years chasing things I no longer desire.

The spark that once burned bright inside me
still shines—

but it shines differently now.

They call me young,

but if they knew what I've seen,

if they felt what I've felt...

they would understand.

I have stopped chasing—

but I have never stopped hoping.

I hope to create something in this life so
beautiful,

so timeless,

that when I am gone,

it will still remain.

It was never about the big white house with the
white fence.

I am a hopeless romantic in a world too heavy to
hold,

lost in my own thoughts with nowhere to go.

The unknown used to terrify me—
now it's the only reason I stand where I stand.

In the unknown, there is hope.
Hope for a life not yet written.
Hope for a love not yet lived.

I want to laugh again.
Watch the sunrise.
Feel the warmth of someone's soul.

The unknown...
once my greatest fear,
now my greatest hope.

We spend our whole lives molded to chase more—
from such a young age,
we're taught to run after the things
we can't carry with us,

the things that will never truly matter.

And I say this with every bone in my body:

there is nothing in this world I would trade for
the scars I carry.

So I accept my fate—

not because it's the only option I have,

but because now—

only now—

I truly understand it.

It was never about the big white house with the
white fence.

It never is.

I thought I understood *fate*...

but I hadn't met him yet.

*I am a hopeless romantic in a world too heavy
to hold,*

lost in my own thoughts with nowhere to go.

LUST, LOVE

I met him in a world that told me my worth

was measured in purity,

in how small I could make myself.

In my family,

a woman's sexuality was a forbidden word.

If you had too much,

you were not pure—

not in their eyes.

My mother was the perfect wife.

One of twelve siblings.

The most beautiful of them all—

long black hair, green eyes, porcelain skin.

A gift from the goddess, they'd say.

Marriage was a man's highest prize.

And the woman?

She was to be pure.

She should have been pure.

That was engraved in me from girlhood:

"Your purity is your greatest gift."

But... why?

Why?

In their eyes, I failed.

Dragged into an engagement

for a mistake I was too young to name.

I was doomed.

I never understood

why something that felt so right,

so innocent to me,

could be so wrong in their eyes.

At eighteen, I broke free—
from a relationship that was never love,
never lust,
only an escape.

I carried that wound for years.
Every love after it carried its shadow.
And when freedom finally kissed my lips,
it tasted both holy and sinful.

Behind closed doors, I became limitless.
I was yours—
to please, to taste, to take.
The lust, the craving...
I didn't have many lovers,
but the few I had
unlocked things I didn't know I longed for.

Skin to skin.
No shame.
No rules.

Yours.

If I gave you my body,
I gave you all of me.
Not just flesh, but trust.

Still, I was robbed—
robbed of what I truly loved
because I was afraid of what they would think.
So many times, I felt wrong.

A hopeless romantic
with so much darkness inside.

So I learned to love.
And I learned to fuck.
And I wanted both.
I needed both.

Control me.
Break me.

And when my body has nothing left to give—

just lay beside me.

Let your skin brush mine.

Let me smell the lust hanging in the air.

For so long,

I didn't think it was possible—

to have both.

Lust. Love.

I was always the good girl.

The one to marry.

To make love.

But I craved lust in the depths of my bones.

My second engagement was a dream.

He was perfect.

He is perfect.

My greatest love.

To them, he was the one.

A beautiful proposal.

Loving parents.

Unconditional warmth.

A kind of love I never imagined I'd receive.

It was love—

pure, sacred love.

But I... was never pure.

How could I stay?

How could I give him the family he dreamed of

when I carried so much shadow inside me?

He wanted to make love.

I wanted to fuck.

And I felt shame.

I felt worthless.

Why am I like this?

Why do I crave what I crave?

Leaving him felt like carving a wound into my own chest.

But I could not stay in a love that touched only part of me.

I needed all of me—

even the shadowed parts.

We are taught to be good wives,

good women.

But if we want too much—

if we speak of the dark cravings inside—

we are judged.

Still, I chose freedom.

But this time... it didn't feel right.

I was hurting.

But I knew I'd never be

who they wanted me to be.

So I had to lose myself

to find myself.

To find you.

You gave me what I'd hidden deep inside.

No judgment.

No wrong.

Only us.

Lust.

Love.

I was yours to please.

And you were mine to ruin.

We fucked.

We loved.

So intoxicated.

So wild.

So right in all the wrong ways.

You proposed after two and a half months.

We married after eight.

Society didn't understand.
I looked innocent—
you looked dark.

But when I surrendered,
you showed me your mind,
and let me lead when I needed to.

Light and darkness.
You and me.

I had both.
Lust.
Love.

Maybe you wanted to fuck,
and I wanted to love.
Or maybe it was the other way around.

Behind our door,
there were no rules.

I was yours.

And no voice from my past could shame me.

Not anymore.

I was a woman.

I was your woman.

And when you give yourself fully—

when someone feeds

your wildest fantasies,

touches your soul

and consumes your body—

you don't forget.

I craved you.

You craved me.

And I still crave that.

When you were gone,

I thought I could never be touched again.

Not like that.

Not by anyone.

Because I was still yours.

Still haunted by your hands,

your hunger.

But now—

the craving is back.

And again, it feels... forbidden.

How can something that made me feel so alive

feel so wrong?

They say,

"You're only human.

You'll crave again.

You're young.

It's okay."

Is it?

Is it really?

It's hard to write what I've tried so long to run
from.

I feel their eyes.

Judging my secrets.

Wanting them buried with me.

But why should I feel shame

for something that made me feel?

So alive.

I am pure.

My heart has always been pure.

It is not wrong.

Lust. Love.

I want both.

I had both.

I crave both.

But craving both is dangerous.
Because once you taste them together—
lust and love in the same breath—
you can't go back to having just one.

And that's when the loop begins—
endless nights with the same question
playing over and over in your mind...

How do we know if it's love?

*To be lust in love— the more dangerous
desire of them all*

*Because when you taste them together you
can't go back to having just one*

How Do We Know If It's Love?

How do we know when it's love?

True love.

It's the question that keeps you awake,

staring at the ceiling,

replaying every kiss, every fight,

every moment you thought you knew the answer—

until you didn't.

What is love?

We spend our whole lives chasing something

that only the heart can truly understand.

Not logic. Not words. Just a feeling.

The greatest gift of all.

I'd be lying if I said it was love at first sight.
I remember the first moment I met him—
casual, easy, fun.
He showed his personality right away.
And somehow... it felt familiar.
Nothing more.

It wasn't that crazy, movie kind of love—
where the whole world stops,
you lock eyes,
and everything suddenly makes sense.

No.
It wasn't love at first sight.
If I'm being honest,
it wasn't even love at all.

It just felt like we'd known each other before.
Like our souls had already crossed paths.

It felt familiar.

They say a woman's intuition
is the most powerful gift she carries.
And this didn't feel like our first life.
Our first love.

When his lips touched mine... it didn't feel new.
It felt like a memory.

But how could that be?

At first, it was easy.
No games. No chase.
It was like we had found each other once again—
in a different lifetime.

But in this one,
the crosses we carried were heavy.
I wanted freedom.
I craved it.

He wanted stability.

He wanted loyalty. Something real.

Sometimes, you don't even realize

the crosses you carry.

Some you pick up along the way,

and some are handed to you

by your own family.

Not out of malice—

but through survival, repetition, pain.

We're all shaped by someone.

We're all molded by something.

And still,

we knew there was something there.

Something real.

Something worth holding on to.

Was it love?

I wish I had learned back then

the things I know now.

But they say poetry is better lived than written.

How can I write about love

if I've never truly loved?

How can I describe the rainbow

if I've never seen color?

If I told you that one day

you'll meet someone who just makes sense—

no games, no chasing—

you might question it.

You might doubt it,

because it's too easy.

Too quiet.

You'll wonder:

Is this love?

Why doesn't it feel like a struggle?

You'll question yourself a hundred times more.

Because love without chaos

can feel unfamiliar.

But that doesn't mean it isn't real.

I couldn't carry his family's wounds.

They were too heavy.

Or maybe... maybe I just wasn't enough.

How can we be so different,

yet still so much the same?

How can I love someone

who never felt love growing up?

How can I love someone

when I've spent most of my life

feeling unworthy of love myself?

But still... something always made me stay.

And fight.

Six lives.

We had six lives.

Maybe that's why this one felt a little easier.

Maybe that's why we always stayed.

Maybe this time the wounds didn't cut as deep.

Maybe we thought...

we could finally do this.

He proposed so fast.

We married even faster.

Not because it was love at first sight—

but because in every single life...

he always leaves.

I've lost him more times than I can count.

And deep down,

I always knew he wasn't mine to keep.

I always knew.

I knew.

And God...
how could I be angry at the same hands
that gave him to me,
for also taking him away?

He was never mine to keep.
And I wasn't his.

We were gifted.
We were given time—
and this time,
time was all we had.

I've accepted that now.
No guilt.
No anger.
No more questions.

I just hope that next time,
when we meet again,
we get a little more time.

Because time...

is the only thing love can't bargain for.

And in the end,

it's the only thing I've ever wished for more of.

So was it love?

It was always love.

A love so deep,

you don't understand it

until it's gone.

And when it was gone, so was I.

Small. Fragile.

Hopeless in the face of love

I could never seem to hold.

Can someone really be worthy of true love...

twice in one lifetime?

HOPELESS

Small. Fragile.
Hopeless in the face of true love.

That's what I've always felt like—
ever since I was a little girl,
craving my mother's acknowledgment,
just wanting to feel loved.

Maybe if I behaved...
maybe if I was a good girl,
my parents would finally see me.

So I tried.
I tried so hard to be that good girl.

No talking back.
Keep your head down.
Find your place in a world
that never really had a place for you.

That's how I learned to survive.

I was afraid to speak my mind—
because I knew there would be consequences.
I'd never be good enough.
How could I be?

Just look at her—
a small, fragile, hopeless little girl
with no voice,
and no one who cared enough to ask
if she was okay.

But how could I be so selfish?
After all, love isn't everything, right?
I had a "healthy" family in the eyes of the world.

Food on the table.

A roof over my head.

Friends.

Then why...

why did it still feel so empty?

Why did I still feel so unloved?

It wasn't her fault.

She didn't have love either.

How could she give me something

she didn't even have for herself?

And now, with a heavy heart,

I understand her—

a young mother, stuck with a loveless husband,

a man who chose every other woman

but the one who stood beside him.

The one who gave him children.

The one who kept the house safe.

The one who worked endless nights
with barely anything,
because she couldn't face the truth:
that one day,
he'd stop choosing us.

I could never blame her
for not knowing how much I needed her love.

It's hard to see the patterns we repeat
until you look back
and find that hopeless little girl.

So small.
So fragile.

I wish I could pick her up,
hold her tight,
and whisper in her ear:

Don't worry.

You'll find love—

the overwhelming love you've always craved.

You will.

But it will come with a price.

I've learned to speak my mind.

To stand my ground.

To choose myself even when it's hard.

I've fallen enough times to know—

there's always a brighter day

hiding behind the dark clouds.

All I've ever wanted in this life

was love.

True love.

My ride or die.

But I didn't know how dangerous that wish
could be.

Because when they leave...

when they leave this earth...

I fall back into that same little girl.

Fragile. Hopeless. Unloved.

In a world where love
doesn't seem to exist anymore.

So when someone new comes along,
I dive in headfirst.
That feeling—
the electricity in the air—
is intoxicating.

I've spent my whole life craving it.
And now that it's here,
I think:
Maybe it's possible.
Maybe I'm worthy of love again.

So I jump—
heart wide open—

hoping this time it's real.

That this time, I won't fight.

Won't raise my voice.

I'll be the good girl.

I'll give my all.

But it still wasn't enough.

Why?

Why?

I held my heart in my hands.

There was nothing left to give.

I didn't ask for much—

just to be held,

to feel the touch of another human being again,

to feel alive.

Now... I don't recognize myself anymore.

The hopeless little girl is back.

She lost her love.

He's not coming back.

And she's alone again.

So she craves more.

She gives more.

She gives everything to someone

who doesn't love her.

Because why should he?

Look at her—

hopeless.

Why would anyone choose me again—

when even I don't recognize who I am?

Be a good girl.

You're my good girl.

Hopeless.

How did I become so hopeless?

I've failed.

Can someone really be worthy of true love...
twice in one lifetime?

Every bone in my body says yes.
Or am I just being selfish?

I feel like I'm back where it all started—
a loop,
a curse,
a loveless little girl
crying through sleepless nights
for a love that wasn't really love.

I already had my great love.
How dare I wish for another?

When I look at her—
hidden behind my eyes—
I realize there's only one way out.

She has to die.

Because if she doesn't...

I'll never meet the woman I was meant to become.

And maybe that's the real reason I've survived this long—

to finally bury her,

and rise as someone unrecognizable

to the ones who broke me.

Becoming

But wait.

Before you let her go...

Before you bury that small, fragile, hopeless little girl—

Let me speak to her.

Because I see her now.

And for the first time in our life—

I'm not ashamed of her.

She is not weak.

She is not broken.

She is not a burden.

She is the reason I survived.

That girl—the one who stayed silent to avoid punishment,

who tried so hard to be "good" so someone might love her—

She didn't fail.

She adapted.

She made it through hell with nothing but sheer will

and the tiniest flicker of hope

that maybe—just maybe—

love would find her one day.

And now I know the truth:

She doesn't have to die.

She doesn't need to be erased.

She needs to be held.

By me.

Because now, finally,

I can be the one she always needed.

Not a mother.

Not a lover.

Me.

I can hold her hand and say:

You're not too much.

You're not broken.

You don't have to earn love anymore.

You never did.

For so long, we believed we had to be small to be
worthy.

Quiet.

Obedient.

A good girl.

But baby—

we were never meant to be small.

We were meant to take up space.

To speak.

To scream.

To sob.

To laugh so loudly it turns heads.

To be messy.

Wild.

Tender.

Soft.

Fierce.

To be all of it.

We are all of it.

I've mistaken survival for love.

I've called silence peace.

I've called neglect strength.

But I'm done.

I'm done being the good girl just to be loved.

Because now—I love her.

The girl who waited.

The girl who begged.

The girl who gave everything and still wasn't chosen.

I choose her.

I choose me.

And I know now—love didn't die when he did.

It felt like it did.

But love is still here.

In the way I show up for myself when no one else does.

In the way I get back up, even when I don't want to.

In the way I write these words

with tears in my eyes

and power in my chest.

And yes—

I believe in love again.

Not just the romantic kind.

But the kind that wraps itself around your soul and says:

You don't have to chase me.

I'm already yours.

Can someone be worthy of true love twice in one lifetime?

Yes.

Absolutely.

And not just twice—

a thousand times over.

Every time you choose yourself.

Every time you speak instead of swallowing your truth.

Every time you say:

No more begging.

No more shrinking.

No more proving.

That's love.

That's rebirth.

This isn't the end of your story.

This is the turning point.

So no, sweet girl—

you don't have to die.

You have to come home.

To me.

And this time,

I won't leave you.

Because now, even in the quiet... I know love isn't gone.

It just changes shape.

And sometimes, it finds a way to reach you—
even beyond the veil.

In Hopelessness, I found Hope—

*Hope of a life not yet written, and Hope of a
love not yet lived*

DAFFODILS

Can love exist beyond the veil?

My body, my soul — everything in me tells me yes.

Because I can still feel him.

He can still hear me.

If I told you that in my wildest dreams I've seen him, spoken to him, touched him...

Would you believe me?

There are things in life that defy explanation.

Sometimes it's not about making sense of it,

but about what it does to your soul.

Have you ever had one of those days

where everything flows —

where you feel touched by luck you can't explain?

I've cried.

Begged.

Screamed myself voiceless.

Pledged my life to the darkness

when the weight was too heavy to carry.

And still — he came to me.

A message in the sky.

A vivid dream.

He touched me.

He pulled me close,

And in that place where words don't need sound,

He whispered: *"Sit still."*

Was it all in my mind?

A desperate hope rising from the edge?

Or was it truly him —

reaching through the veil to keep me from falling?

I feel his energy wrap around me

in moments I don't think I can survive.

Maybe it's because I'm not strong enough —

and he knows.

Or maybe... maybe I am blessed

to receive a love

that still travels light-years just to reach me.

I know what I've seen.

I know what I've felt.

I carry these moments like sacred treasures —

too precious to speak aloud,

for fear the world might steal them,

and with them, the only reason I'm still breathing.

Another life...

In another life...

I've been on my knees
more times than I'd ever admit.
Pledged my soul
more than anyone should have to.

"You're such a strong woman."

They say that like it's a badge of honor.
But strength doesn't feel like this.
Strength doesn't feel like
begging God to bring you back,
or whispering to the dark,
"I can't do this. Please don't make me."

No one was there to hear me.
But somehow — he always was.

His voice, his presence,
woven into the pain like a thread of light.
Each fall taught me something.
Each rise came with a lesson.

The falls grew heavier.

But rising? It became familiar. Not easier — just expected.

I don't feel strong.

I've just stopped bleeding when I should've.

Not because I'm brave —

but because eventually, everything ends.

Even the life we had together.

So I fall to my knees again,

and offer the life I still have

to the one who still reaches for me.

Am I strong?

Or have all my prayers been heard?

"I sent you daffodils in a pretty string... the veil doesn't stop us - it just changes how I reach you.'

And in that moment, I know—

even if I can't touch you in this life,

there's a place where I can.

A place where our love lives free.

WHERE OUR LOVE LIVES FREE

My love,

I can still feel you.
even here.
even now.

The veil may keep us in separate realms,
But it hasn't taken you from me.
It only changed the way you reach me.

Your presence is stitched into my days —
in the quiet moments when the world forgets me,
in the soft ache that follows me to sleep,
in the air that shifts when I whisper your name.

I've tried for so long to put this past year into words,

but everything I write feels too small for the weight of it.

The days have been heavy,

the nights even heavier.

Sometimes it feels like I'm wandering through a dream that's too quiet...

too empty.

It's hard to find purpose when life refuses to hand you one.

So many dreams have been stolen—

shut down by hands that only know how to take.

Family who turned into strangers.

Friends who became something colder than enemies.

I still don't understand why.

I don't know how to keep seeing the light in people

when all I've been shown is betrayal.

But somewhere deep in my heart,

I know this pain is the beginning of something else.

A rebirth.

A new bloodline.

A curse broken.

I won't let what happened to us harden me.

I won't let it turn me into the kind of person

who breaks others just to feel whole.

The patterns in our families run deep,

but I will not carry them any further.

We get to decide who we are—

not the ones who came before us.

You taught me that it's not about what we accomplish in this life—

it's about the way our love imprints itself

onto the hearts that survive us.

And yet... I've seen grief turned into a *weapon*.

I've seen it make people cruel.

I've seen it take their hands and turn them, into claws.

They say it's one of the hardest things in this world

to truly change who you are.

But I did.

I had to.

My pain dragged me into a darkness no one should ever have to walk through—

and in that place, I decided:

If I'm going to survive this,

I will not come out the same.

I built myself into a woman I had only ever imagined before—

the way she stands,

the way she moves,

the compassion she offers even to those who cannot return it.

She became the change she wanted to see in the world.

And still... when life swallows her again,

when she's back on her knees with silent screams caught in her chest,

when the tears burn and the hours blur,

when her hands shake as she prays that someone—anyone—will come save her,

the truth always arrives like a blade:

No one is coming.

No one can hear her.

No one ever will.

And in those moments, my love,

the question always finds me:

Is this the end?

Is this how I leave?

Would anyone notice tomorrow?

Has my pain grown so deep that the thought of ending it

feels like a bittersweet dream?

There's a voice in the dark sometimes—

a soft, dangerous one—

promising peace.

An end to the ache.

An end to the weight.

And maybe...

maybe I have made peace with whatever fate comes.

I've been ready since the day you were taken from me—

the only true love my soul ever knew.

But even in the dark, I had love.

And if I can't feel it in this life again,

then I will carry it like a flame in my chest

until my last breath.

Because you don't stop loving someone when they're gone.

If anything, you love them more.

The pain. The tears. I take them all.

And next time—

I will love even harder.

Because now I know how quickly it can all be gone.

Love changed me.

Pain changed me.

I don't fully know who I am now.

But I know who I'm not.

The girl I used to be died with you.

That version of us lives on somewhere else—

in a universe untouched by loss.

A place where our love is whole and unbroken.

Where we dance under the sky like the first time we met.

Where the song never ends.

No one can touch us there.

Because in an infinite universe,

our love lives free.

And that—

that is what lifts me from the ground.

That is why I choose to keep breathing.

I might not have you here in the way I want,

but when I close my eyes and go still,

I can find you.

I can slip into that other place

where you are waiting for me.

The place where our love lives free.

Where it always will.

My diamond love...the rarest and most precious
of them all.

You can't buy it.

You have to search for it, work for it, fight for
it—

and even, only the lucky ever find it.

If I had to choose between all the gold, all the
wealth, all the treasure of the world...

I would still choose you.

Every time.

LOVE OR MONEY?

I would be lying if I said money isn't important.

But one day, you will stop, look around, and realize—none of it matters, not in the way you thought it would.

And in that moment, it will all make sense.

A big house with too many empty rooms.

A fast car with nowhere to go.

Lonely dinners at the nicest tables.

I had all of that... and still, I would have traded it all for a seven-dollar sandwich in the park with you, watching our dogs play.

Because the truth is, money can buy comfort, but it can't buy meaning.

And it can never buy the kind of love that makes you feel alive.

When I close my eyes, I feel the pain carved into my heart.

I miss the way it felt to be in your arms.

The sound of your heartbeat.

The smell of your skin.

The warmth of your body against mine.

The long talks about nothing and everything.

Talking about a future we were never going to have together.

Dreaming about the things I would only achieve without you.

I had to lose you to realize I had everything.

I had to lose you to realize you were my everything.

A home without love is just a house.

A race car without a driver is just a machine.

One day, you will look around and feel the same ache I carry inside me as I write these words.

I just hope life is kind to you—and that you realize it before it's too late, like it was for me.

It's a strange truth... that I had to lose you to become a better version of myself.

I had to lose you to truly find myself.

I understand life a little better now.

I might not have all the answers or know exactly where to go from here...

But I know one thing with absolute certainty:

If I had a thousand lives, I would always choose love.

A diamond is only as special as love — both rare and precious.

Finding your person is the greatest gift someone can achieve in a lifetime.

And just like a raw diamond isn't perfect—love isn't either.

You don't throw away or replace a diamond because it's not flawless.

A raw diamond, in the hands of someone who understands its worth, can become the most valuable treasure in the world. But it takes time, care, and knowing when to be gentle and when to be strong.

Diamonds are not found just anywhere.

They're discovered in the hardest places—deep beyond the surface, past rock bottom—where all hope seems gone.

Only there, in the darkest places, can you find the rarest and most powerful stone: raw, uncut, and real.

Your love is your raw diamond.

Only a foolish man would throw it away, chasing something "perfect."

I found my raw, uncut diamond love once.

It was the most precious thing I ever had.

At times, I took it for granted.

I questioned my own feelings.

But every time I truly stopped to look, I saw it.

That spark. The look.

The spark in your eyes.

The way you looked at me.

Even now, I can't find the words to describe what I felt every time you looked at me that way.

In our last moments together, as I looked down at you, I saw that same spark. 'The look'.

And life, in its strange mercy, allowed that to be the last thing I saw—before waking up to a new life without it.

The look...

If I had a thousand lives, I would always choose love.

Sometimes, when I close my eyes and make the world go quiet, I can feel you again.

I can hear your heartbeat.

Smell your scent.

It consumes me in a way I can't explain.

It's the moment time stops—and I have you again.

Just for a second.

And then, as it always does, it fades.

I open my eyes to a world where you no longer exist.

And I feel powerless.

But it's like you knew.

Like life knew I needed you—just for a moment.

I needed to remember what it felt like to be loved.

And so you appear.

Not to stay.

But to remind me.

To remind me of what it means to feel *love*.

And yet... when the moment faded,

I was left with questions.

Was it real?

Was it only my mind?

That's when the signs began.

Beyond The Veil

Once, I thought the questions would destroy me.

I questioned love.

I questioned myself.

I questioned everything—

because of the noise in my head.

The first time it happened, I thought I was crazy.

Maybe I was.

But I was so far gone, I didn't care what people thought.

I didn't think I would live a long life anyway.

So when the signs appeared,

that's all I saw.

And I embraced them—every single one—

without caring what anyone might say.

I felt connected.

Lucky.

Afraid.

Afraid it could all vanish in a second.

Afraid that if I spoke, if I told anyone, it would disappear.

Afraid—because I had already lost you once.

And yet I had you,

in a way I couldn't explain.

Afraid the signs would leave me.

But they never did.

I know that now.

I know what I've seen.

I know how to reach you.

In strange, mysterious ways,

you always come back to me.

Signs.

In a world full of noise,

where we're taught to question everything,

you whisper: *Sit still.*

I'm not here to tell you what's right or wrong,

what's true or false.

But I'll tell you a secret:

Sometimes, when life gives you the kind of love
that lives beyond the veil,

you're given a thread.

A key.

A doorway between realms.

It won't make sense.

You'll be afraid to share it.

The world will insist it's all in your head.

But if you're like me—

a curious soul with nothing left to lose—

you'll dive in.

You'll cling to that thread with everything you have.

And the more you trust the signs,

the more you learn to navigate between realms.

You are not crazy.

We are not crazy.

I know what I've seen.

I know what I've touched.

I know what I've heard.

Not every day.

Not every night.

But always when it mattered most.

You knew when I needed you.

Maybe this is the most controversial chapter of all.

People will call it fairy tales.

They'll try to decode it.

Dismiss it.

Erase it.

But they can't.

Because the waters hold the secret.
And no one can take that away from me.

I was once afraid of the dark.
Afraid of demons.
Afraid of losing you.
Afraid the signs would fade.

But now I know better.
The signs were always there.
The thread was always there.
And I will never let it go again.

Beyond the veil—
where love lives untouched,
where demons cannot reach.

I was given the greatest gift of all.

And it was always love.

I had to lose you to know.

But now I will never forget.

I will hold onto this thread—

and no one can take it away from me.

Not even *you*.

So find love.

Find true love—

the kind of love you wish to receive in this life.

Give it to a friend.

To your family.

To the one you cherish most.

Because when they're gone—

in the split of a second—

they will know everything there is to know.

They will see your true intentions.

They will know your deepest secrets.

They will know the real *you.*

And they will have the power to guide you.

So choose love.

Always love.

Because love is what survives beyond the veil.

Be smart.

Be resilient.

It's okay to question.

But never let the questions run your whole world,

your whole mind.

INFINITE POSSIBILITIES

We spend our whole lives questioning ourselves,

trying to make sense of everything... and
nothing at all.

My mother was right in her own way—

"You ask too many questions," she used to say.

I guess that's what I thought survival was.

If I asked enough questions,

if I thought through every possible scenario,

maybe life would be easier.

But it never was.

It never is.

Nothing can prepare you for the weight of grief.

There are no words strong enough for it.

I've always been curious—hungry for answers—

but this whole time, I'd missed something simple, yet so precious.

The answers were right in front of me.

I thought life was a *puzzle* to solve before the clock ran out.

I was wrong.

The truth was in every moment we lived,

in every love, every loss, every ache.

And still—I missed it.

We're here to feel.

To love.

To rage.

To lose.

How can you learn to master your anger if you've never been angry?

How can you understand love without knowing its absence?

The answers have always been here.

But humans... we keep asking,

keep trying to make sense of everything—

as if life owes us an explanation.

For the longest time, I thought grief would be the end of me.

I wanted it. I made peace with it.

Why stay in a world where nothing felt worth staying for?

I've been closer to the edge than I care to admit.

It became my safe place.

Because I knew—I could end it at any second.

That kind of power is dangerous.

And yet, I stayed.

Even in my darkest moments,

there were still questions running through my mind.

Until one day, they stopped.

When you sit in nothing but darkness,
with no one who can hear you,
with pain so deep it's carved into your chest...
it changes you.

It's not about the questions anymore.
Not everything has to mean something.
Not everything needs to be solved.

I only know my reality.
And in my story, I am my own hero.
I can't change anyone else's ending—not even
yours.
I can only hope for a better one.

So no more questions.
I've spent my life chasing meaning in everything,
but now... I choose the unknown.
I'll always be that curious little girl,
full of dreams and hungry for answers,

but now I give my pain the time it deserves—
and then I let it go.

I will always face my demons.
I will invite them in, but never to stay.

I can't promise I'll never be hurt again.
I can't promise I'm completely healed.
The worst thing that ever happened to me
was also my rebirth—
the moment I became a stronger, sharper,
more brilliant version of myself.

And still, I like the unknown.

The unknown is a bittersweet dream.
I'd rather make a bargain with it
than try to script my own future.
Because if I surrender to God's plan—
to the universe—
there are infinite possibilities.

I don't know how many times I'll fall in love in one lifetime.

I don't know if I'll have the big white house with the white fence,

or the wild, intoxicating love that keeps me up at night.

I don't know.

And how exciting is that?

When I began this journey,

it was pure survival—

but not the kind I'd always known.

This was survival from myself.

It was my way of leaving something behind

in case I surrendered to the darkness.

The thought still lingers in the corner of my mind.

The demons are still here.

I see them.

But I live in the unknown now.

Infinite possibilities.
It's not a question—
it's an affirmation.

That little girl who drove her mother crazy
with too many questions—
the hopeless romantic—
she is still here.
She is the best version of me.
And I will always choose her.

Infinite possibilities.
That's where I'll leave you.

Afraid of the dark, I once was.
But now... I write.

IMMORTALIVE

Writing never came easy to me.

I was born in another country, another language.

Words stumbled.

And I've struggled to capture how I truly felt in the moment.

So I wrote.

I've written out of anger.

Out of love.

Out of pain.

And now... out of survival.

The world has always made me feel misunderstood.

I stumble through words to express what I feel—

because it was never really about the words.

Words can be meaningless.

If I translated this whole book into Portuguese—word by word—

it wouldn't carry the same meaning.

It wouldn't make you feel what I feel.

My whole life,

I've tried to control my words,

to control my emotions.

To feel less.

To express less.

But we are here to feel.

To love.

To appreciate.

To experience—

the good and the bad.

To lose... and to gain.

Life is so simple,

and yet so complicated.

Some people spend their whole lives trying to solve it—

like it's a puzzle.

But it isn't.

Think of string theory.

For generations and generations scientists have given their entire lives to decode it.

A simple string.

A thread.

They say string theory is like knowing music exists,

but not having ears sensitive enough

to hear its faintest notes.

And maybe that's the beauty of it—

not to decode,

not to prove,

but simply... to know it exists.

That's how I feel about the thread I hold to the veil.

I can't explain it.

There are no words.

But it is real.

As real as string theory itself.

A mystic string that isn't meant to be decoded.

Like the demons I've seen.

Not the kind you imagine hiding under your bed,

but in people—

in the bargains they make without even realizing.

Your youth traded for wealth.

Your time traded for wealth.

Every interaction... a transaction.

And those bargains bleed into the world we live in now.

A world where technology advances day by day,

where robots can replace humans in so many ways.

But they will never replace us.

Because they will never feel.

They will never know grief.

They will never know love.

They will never know hope.

Emotions are what make us human.

Emotions are what get us up

when life feels hopeless.

Edward Witten.

Leonard Susskind.

Juan Maldacena.

Great scientists who spent their whole lives

trying to prove string theory.

Imagine that—

spending a lifetime chasing something you can't explain...

but you know it's real.

That's how I feel

about the string that ties me to the veil.

...

On that morning.

The last morning.

I remember everything.

The warmth of the winter sun.

The birds singing.

His hoodie wrapped around me—

one of the many I loved to wear.

It was a perfect morning for most.

For me, it was my worst nightmare.

I looked down at him with so much guilt.

Knowing I couldn't save him.

My hands shaking.
My tears unstoppable.

And in that moment—
I made a promise.
To him.
To myself.

I would never spend the rest of my life
chasing after things
I cannot carry beyond the veil.

Instead,
I would love again.
I would laugh again.
I would enjoy a good meal
with good company—
with people who are not here to bargain.
A new chapter.

A new book.

Yet to be written.

Yet to be lived.

I walk into the unknown,

holding only the string of life.

No bargains to be made.

Just a gift.

A gift left by the one who loved me
unconditionally.

And now I know—

you're never truly gone.

Immortalive.

The love that lives beyond the veil.

Immortalive (adj./noun)

Pronunciation: /ih-MOR-tah-liv/

Definition:

1. A love that is both immortal and alive — existing beyond death, time, and the physical world.

2. The unbroken bond that continues to breathe in eternity, living still beyond the veil.

3. A state of eternal connection between souls, transcending mortality and remaining forever vibrant.

Usage in a sentence:

• "Ours is an Immortalive love — alive in this world, and eternal in the next."

• "She believed in Immortalive, the love that lives beyond the veil."

THE CLUES I LEFT BEHIND

A veil.

I don't wish you to understand it.

I don't wish you to believe it.

I don't wish you to know what I know.

Many of you might have picked up this book as a tribute to my husband.

Or maybe because you wanted to know me a little better.

Or maybe you were just wandering through a library one day,

searching for a dark fairytale that might give you hope.

And as I carry you through these chapters,

letting my story consume you—

some of you will think:

What a beautiful fairytale.

How could it not be?

She found her soulmate in a world full of demons.

And when he was gone,

he left her with the greatest gift of all—

a thread, a key,

that connects her to the veil where love cannot be broken.

Some of you will believe this is the perfect ending to a love story.

But others—

others will question.

You'll think it's nothing more than desire.

A placebo for the things I could not explain.

And in truth... I want both to be true.

Because I don't wish you to know what I know.

I don't wish you to see what I've seen,
or feel what I have felt.

I want you to question.
I want you to debate.
I want you to dream.

Because if you understand this book—
then you know.
And that is not how a fairytale should end.

How can a fairytale end like this?

That I had my greatest love,
my soulmate—my mate—
and now, as I walk this earth,
knowing that
I will never be loved the way he loved me.
I will never feel what I felt.
I will never again see the look.
The look—the spark only he carried.

That in his last moments,

he left me a thread to hold.

Something I could grasp when life became too heavy.

A way to love again in silence.

But also a reminder:

that every time I give my love to someone new,

I am bargaining with destiny.

Because the truth is—

their soulmate might live elsewhere on this earth.

But mine?

Mine lives beyond it.

So no—

I don't want you to understand this book. Not yet.

I want you to live a full life.

I want you to see this as a fairytale.

I want you to chase love at all costs.

This book is meant to guide you—

to a better version of yourself.

To embrace the unknown.

To heal the wounds that keep you small.

To never give up,

even when the world goes dark,

even when you are on your knees, begging, pledging

Because we are here to feel.

Nothing more.

And only then—

when you are old,

when your hands are wrinkled,

when you've lived a meaningful life and found your own soulmate—

only then do I want you to truly understand what I've written.

Only then.

So yes—please, question this book.

Tell me I'm wrong.

Tell me I've only been dreaming.

That the veil is just a metaphor—

a story my mind created to survive.

Fight or flight.

Prefrontal cortex suppression.

Dorsal vagal shutdown.

These are all real.

Well-studied in neuroscience and psychology.

That I've dived into,

trying to make sense of what I hold in my hands.

Because sometimes,

making sense feels like a softer ending.

So please—tell me I'm wrong.

Because for once in my life,

I don't want to be right.

I've spent years trying to prove when I'm right.

Arguing. Debating.

Losing friends.

Making my mother mad.

Always needing to be right.

And now—

for the first time—

I want to be wrong.

I want this to be only a fairytale.

I want to leave you with hope.

I don't want you to understand this book.

I don't want you to catch on to the clues I've hidden inside every chapter

like a secret code,

meant only for the ones who walk among us carrying the truth.

Three.

Three times.

I have been wrong in my life.

And this—

this is the one I have wished for.

Because truth has a cost.

And it is a cost I would never wish upon my worst enemy.

Proverbs 24:17–18. Romans 12:17–19. Matthew 5:44.

I spent so many of my younger years following my mother to church,

or going with my father to Mass.

I never felt fully connected to their religion.

To be honest, I still don't.

But in a way that would be controversial to them,

I understand those verses better now than I ever did.

And even today,

if I were to explain to my parents what I've seen,

what I know,

what those verses truly mean—

they would tell me: '*You are wrong*.'

And with a smile on my face,

I would be glad

Because that means

they don't know the truth.

and so I leave the rest unsaid— not for the world,

but for him.

for the one who carried the truth with me

until the very end.

THE LAST LETTER

Love Bug,

⌘

As I stare at this blank paper, trying to find words to write to you one more time one more letter, our last letter I realize how hard it is. Maybe because everything I ever wanted to tell you, I already have. And somehow, that gives me peace.

So many times I silently asked myself: what will become of me when you're no longer here? I lived with that thought in my mind for so many years, more than anyone should ever have to.

I wanted to be wrong so many times.

But I've always carried this gift, this blessing, this curse.

It's like I could sense it. I knew when something was wrong. I always had that instinct. My whole life.

And deep down, I knew you weren't mine to keep. I knew we wouldn't grow old side by side.

I always knew.

Part of me even wanted to leave at times

I didn't know if I had what it would take to stay.

But I could never have done that to you. Never.

I had seen your pain. Felt your sacrifices. Watched your drive. Your endless sleepless nights.

So I stayed.

I stayed even though I knew this would be the end of me too.

I'm not angry. I'm not mad. I could never be.

This was my choice, and I'm glad I made it.

I had made peace with that choice a long time ago.

I just wasn't expecting this side of the bargain, to break me to my knees.

But it's a relief to know you have peace now.

It's a relief to know you lived the life you lived.

And I was blessed to be even a small part of it.

Thank you for being my best friend.

Thank you for loving me.

Thank you for teaching me how to forgive, how to be kind, how to live life to the fullest, and never ever be afraid.

You healed more parts of me than you ever broke.

I don't know where I'm going.

I don't know how much time I have left.

I don't have answers to the questions that run through my mind.

I only know this: I want to be strong enough to stay a little longer. And I wish to make you proud.

Someone recently asked me if I thought you were just a chapter in my life.

But you're not.

You are the whole damn fucking book.

A book I still have yet to finish writing.

I hope our next life is easier. And in that life, I hope we have more time together.

Time.

It's the only thing I wish I had more of with you.

I promise to work on my traumas and my insecurities in this life. To heal my deepest wounds without harming anyone else.

I will love again. I will laugh again.

And maybe, one day, I'll even have a new family.

I'll live a full life. A meaningful life.

I don't regret anything. I'm here to learn.

I'm here to grow. To break the curse.

And when my time comes, when I close my eyes for the very last time, I hope the first thing I see... is you.

Always Yours,

Francy

"Come back to me.

Come find me one more time. For one more life."

ACKNOWLEDGEMENTS

Nothing in this life is done alone. I stand where I stand today because of the people who have walked beside me, lifted me, and loved me.

To the love of my life, my soulmate, Nathan Rossi—my greatest love, my true love. You loved me unconditionally when I had nothing to offer but myself. Even though writing this book took the life out of me, I am beyond thankful for the honor of being your wife. Everything I create, everything I grow into, I do with the desire to make you proud. Seeing this book come alive is proof of how far I've come since the first page I ever wrote. I carry only pure gratitude for you, and for being chosen to love you in this lifetime.

To my best friend, Janis Tello. I could not be standing here without you. You showed up for me on the worst day of my life—without a phone call, without an invitation, you just came. You picked me up off the ground when I didn't know if I could go on. You believed in me when I couldn't see anything worth believing in myself. You once told me you knew I'd be fine, that I had what it takes to survive another day. You saw something in me I couldn't yet see, and I have carried that faith with me into every word I've written. I will forever be thankful for your love, your presence, and your friendship.

To the mystery hidden between the lines of this book—your chapter is unforgettable. Thank you for reminding me that love can find us again, even if only lived inside one heart.

Inspiration for the quote "I sent you daffodils in a pretty string..." from page 69, came from one of the many songs that mended my heart: Another Love by Tom Odell.

And finally, to Love itself—the greatest gift of them all. Thank you for letting me love again. And maybe, if I'm worthy, one day, love will choose me again.